TGIF

TO GENTLEMEN IN FORM

M MRITHIKA SANTHOSHINI

ISBN 979-888503330-5

TO ALL MEN WHO ARE MANLY INSIDE OUT

Contents

Contents

About The Author

M Mrithika Santhoshini is an Author, Co Director, Lyricist, Translator and Artivist. She works in Film Industry from 2010 as a dialogue writer, co-director and costume designer, have translated three Tamil poetry books of contemporary poets' into English. Her first book 'WAW' What A Woman containing fifty one quotes on feminism was published on Women's Day, 2021. She has authored two more books 'Take A Bow' and 'Giggles'. This is her fourth book. She has done her Master's in English and lives in Coimbatore with her parents and pets.

For more information follow her on

thewordgardener

Mittutweety

CHAPTER ONE

GOD

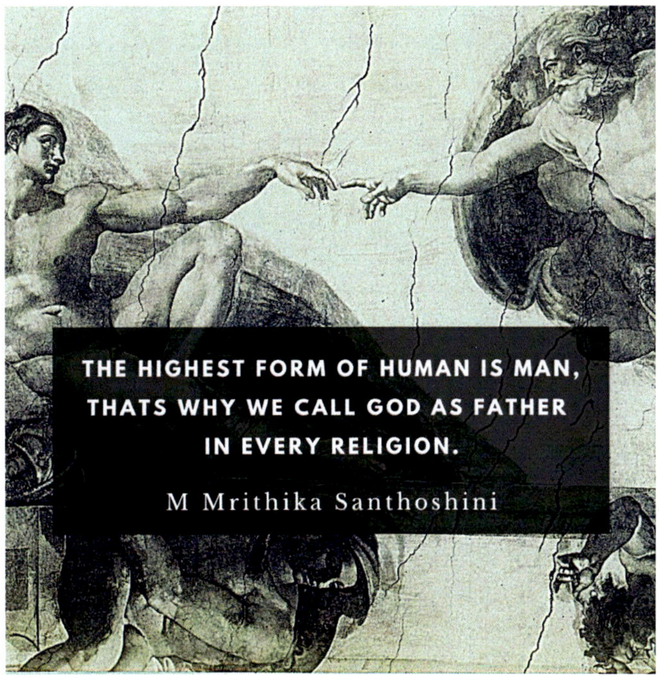
THE HIGHEST FORM OF HUMAN IS MAN,
THATS WHY WE CALL GOD AS FATHER
IN EVERY RELIGION.
M Mrithika Santhoshini

CHAPTER TWO

MAN AND WOMAN

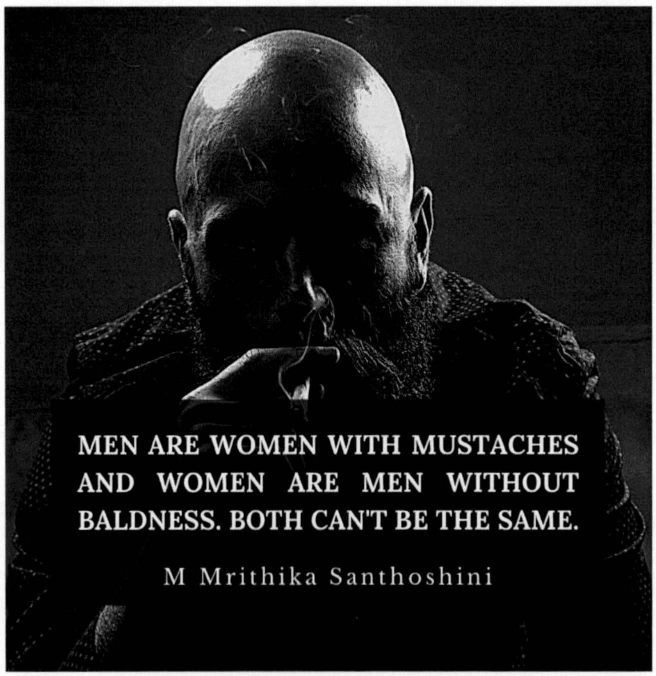
MEN ARE WOMEN WITH MUSTACHES AND WOMEN ARE MEN WITHOUT BALDNESS. BOTH CAN'T BE THE SAME.
M Mrithika Santhoshini

CHAPTER THREE

ELIGIBLE BACHELOR

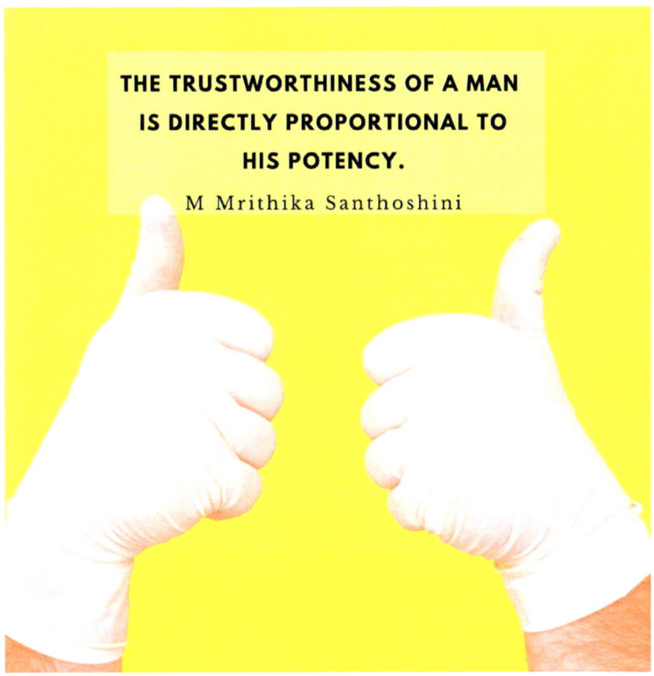
THE TRUSTWORTHINESS OF A MAN
IS DIRECTLY PROPORTIONAL TO
HIS POTENCY.
M Mrithika Santhoshini

CHAPTER FOUR

HUSTLER

REAL MEN DON'T QUIT.
M Mrithika Santhoshini

CHAPTER FIVE

CLEAN MAN

NEVER UNDERESTIMATE
A MAN IN FORMALS.
M Mrithika Santhoshini

CHAPTER SIX

FEARLESS MAN

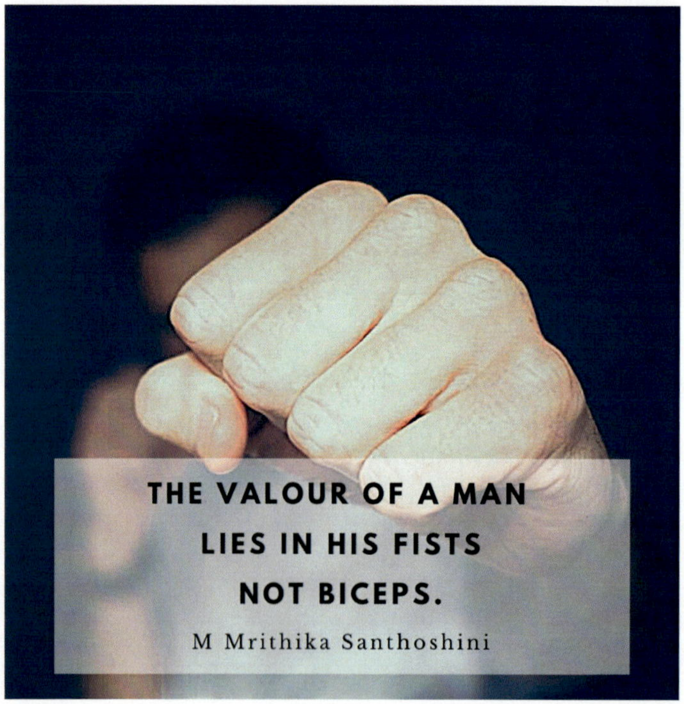
THE VALOUR OF A MAN
LIES IN HIS FISTS
NOT BICEPS.
M Mrithika Santhoshini

CHAPTER SEVEN

THOUGHTFUL MAN

DECISIVENESS IS THE ONLY INGREDIENT
WHICH MAKES THE MAN, A HERO.
M Mrithika Santhoshini

CHAPTER EIGHT

IMMATURE MAN

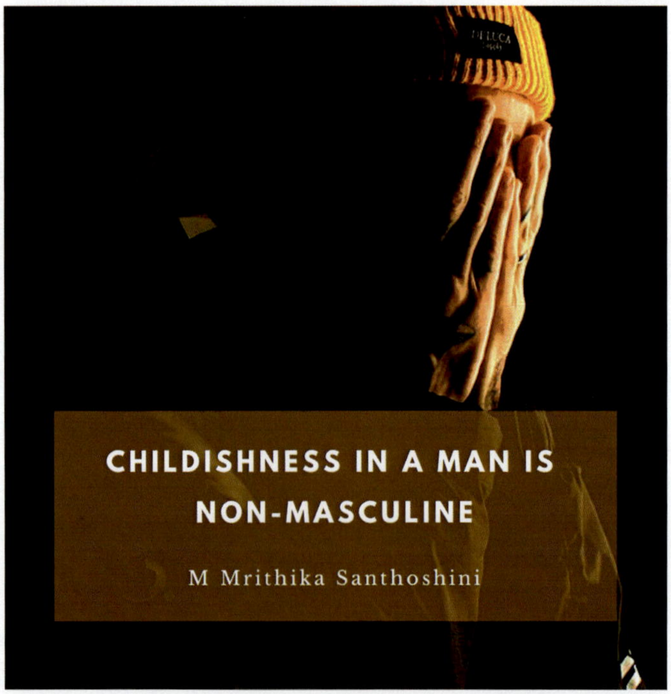
CHILDISHNESS IN A MAN IS NON-MASCULINE
M Mrithika Santhoshini

CHAPTER NINE

HAPPY MAN

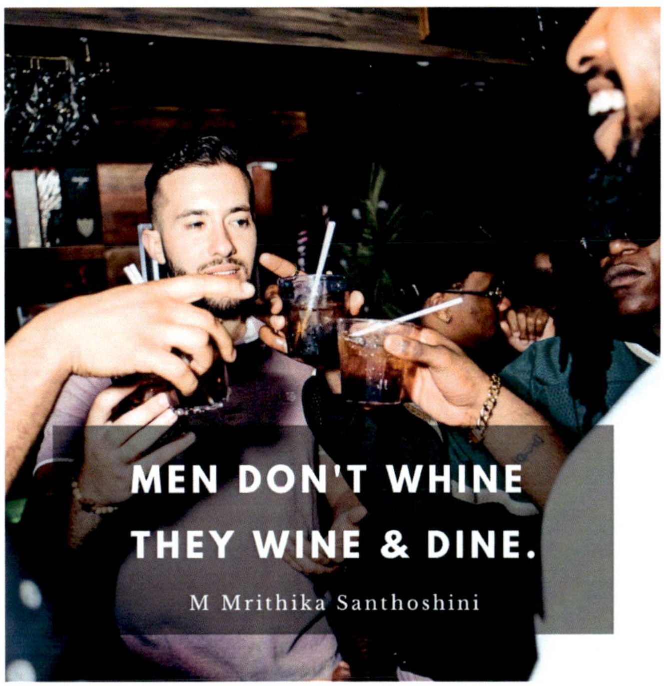
MEN DON'T WHINE
THEY WINE & DINE.
M Mrithika Santhoshini

CHAPTER TEN

COOL MAN

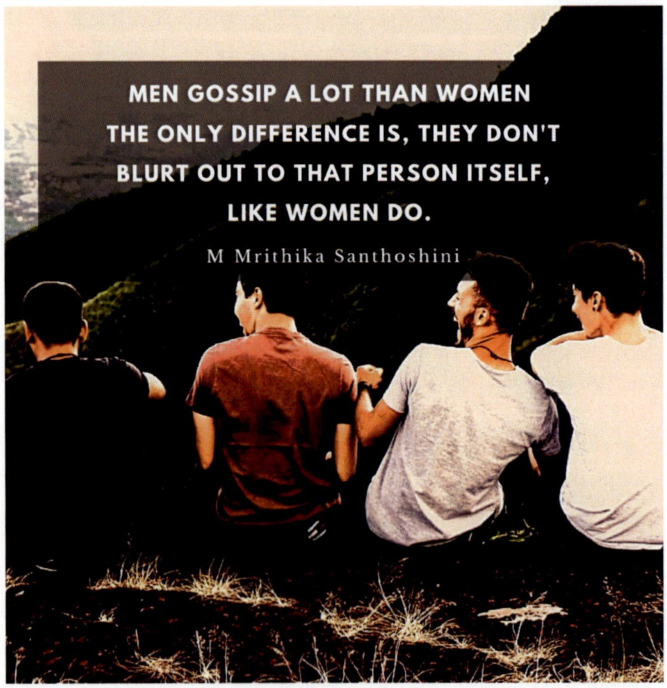

MEN GOSSIP A LOT THAN WOMEN
THE ONLY DIFFERENCE IS, THEY DON'T
BLURT OUT TO THAT PERSON ITSELF,
LIKE WOMEN DO.
M Mrithika Santhoshini

CHAPTER ELEVEN

MAN OF PRINCIPLES

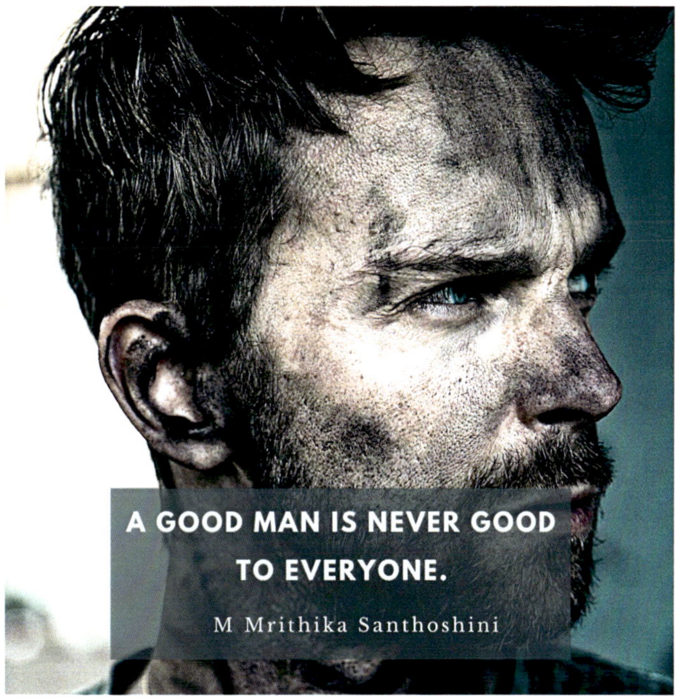
A GOOD MAN IS NEVER GOOD
TO EVERYONE.
M Mrithika Santhoshini

CHAPTER TWELVE

HARDWORKING MAN

MEN DON'T CRY, THEY SWEAT.
M Mrithika Santhoshini

CHAPTER THIRTEEN

MILLIONAIRE

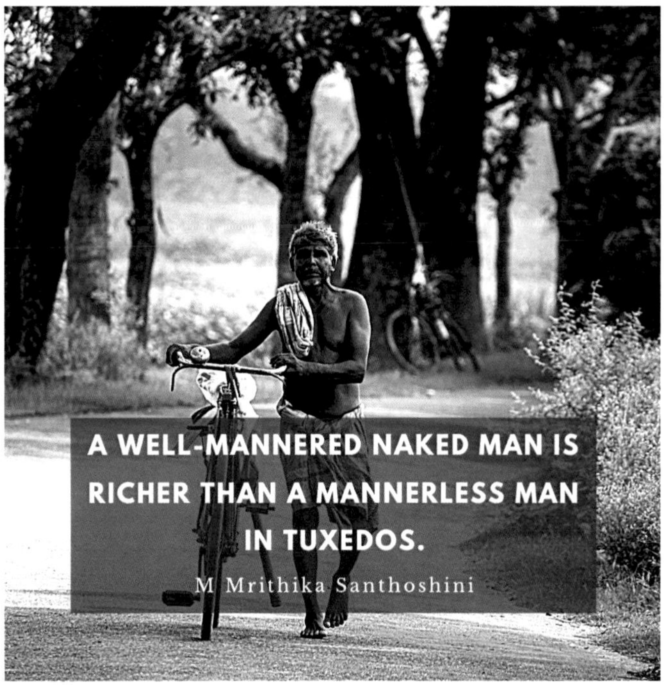
A WELL-MANNERED NAKED MAN IS RICHER THAN A MANNERLESS MAN IN TUXEDOS.
M Mrithika Santhoshini

CHAPTER FOURTEEN

MACHO MAN

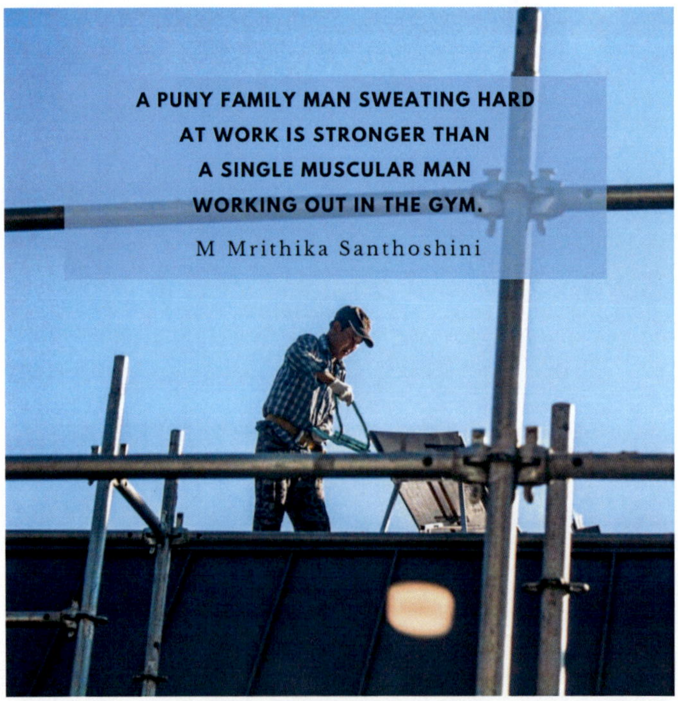
A PUNY FAMILY MAN SWEATING HARD
AT WORK IS STRONGER THAN
A SINGLE MUSCULAR MAN
WORKING OUT IN THE GYM.
M Mrithika Santhoshini

CHAPTER FIFTEEN

POWERFUL MAN

MAN CAN BUILD MUSCLE BUT
THE POWER OF A MAN
IS NEVER BUILT IN A GYM.
M Mrithika Santhoshini

CHAPTER SIXTEEN

SUPERHERO

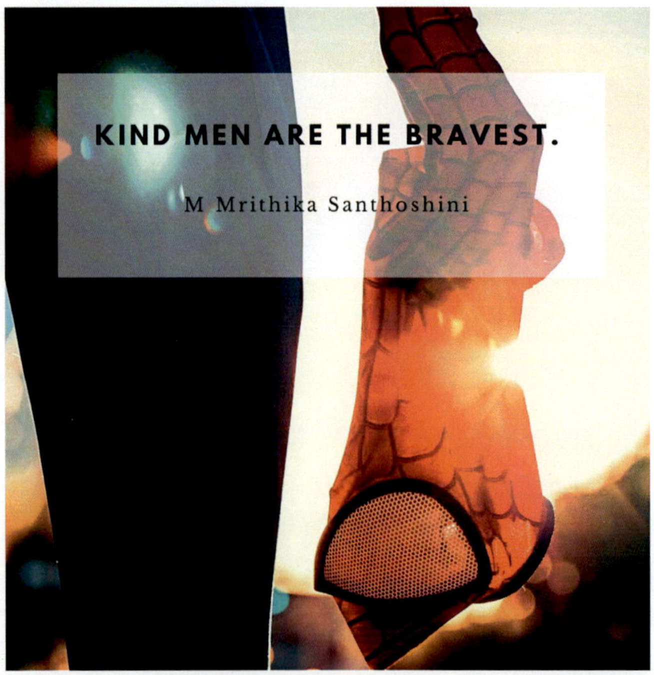
KIND MEN ARE THE BRAVEST.
M Mrithika Santhoshini

CHAPTER SEVENTEEN

HERO

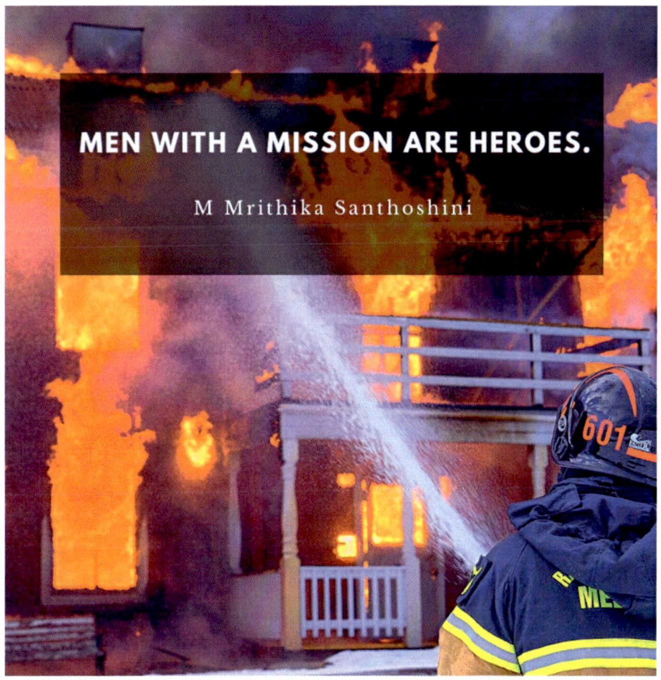
MEN WITH A MISSION ARE HEROES.
M Mrithika Santhoshini
601

CHAPTER EIGHTEEN

SUPERSTAR

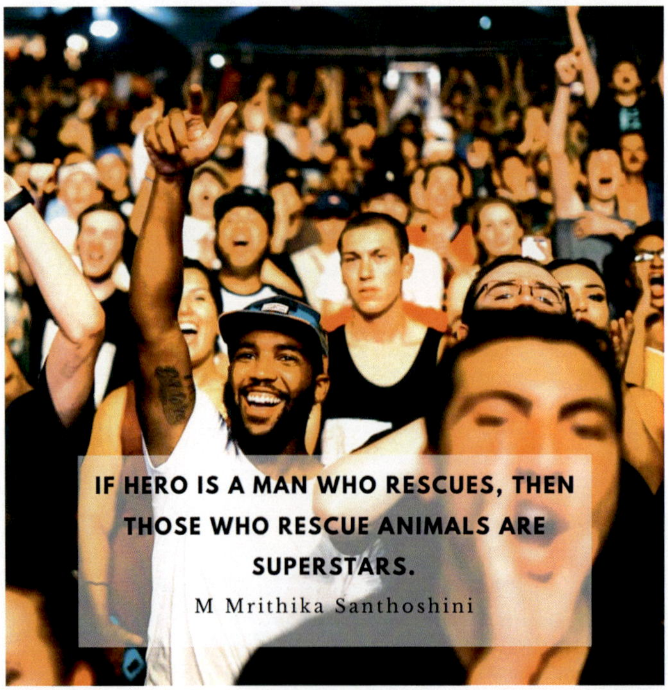
IF HERO IS A MAN WHO RESCUES, THEN THOSE WHO RESCUE ANIMALS ARE SUPERSTARS.
M Mrithika Santhoshini

CHAPTER NINETEEN

GREYHAIRED MAN

MEN WHO DON'T HIDE THEIR GREY
NEVER GROW
OLD.
M Mrithika Santhoshini

CHAPTER TWENTY

EVER'GREY' MAN

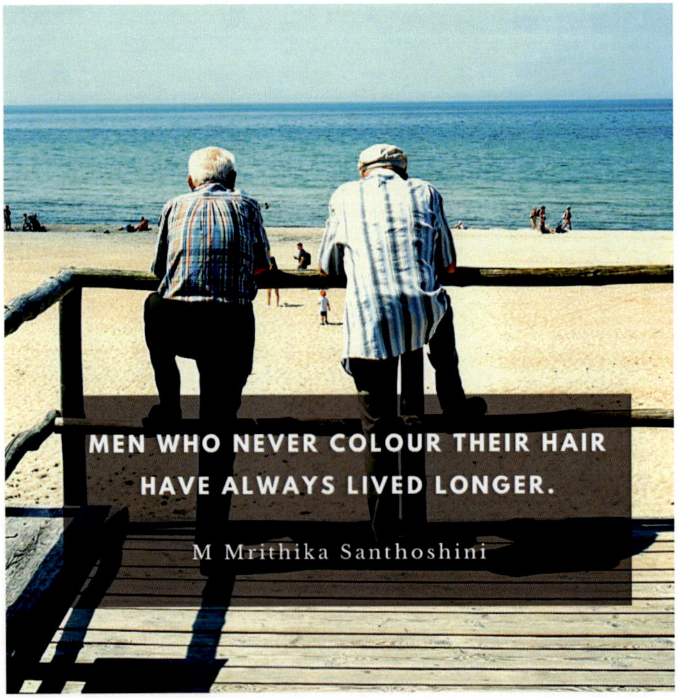
MEN WHO NEVER COLOUR THEIR HAIR
HAVE ALWAYS LIVED LONGER.
M Mrithika Santhoshini

CHAPTER TWENTY-ONE

HUMOUROUS MAN

A MAN WHO LAUGHS A LOT
HAS GRIEF IN HIM MORE THAN
A WOMAN THAT CONSTANTLY CRIES.
M Mrithika Santhoshini

CHAPTER TWENTY-TWO

RUDE MAN

RUDE MEN REQUIRE
MORE LOVE.
M Mrithika Santhoshini

CHAPTER TWENTY-THREE

REAL MAN

REAL MEN NEVER FEEL INTIMIDATED
BY THE INTELLIGENCE OF A WOMAN.
M Mrithika Santhoshini

CHAPTER TWENTY-FOUR

DAUNTLESS MAN

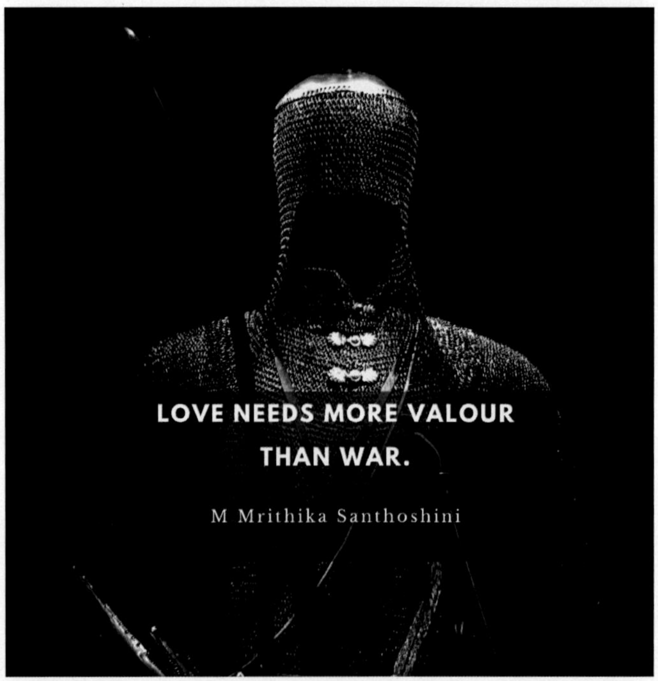
LOVE NEEDS MORE VALOUR
THAN WAR.
M Mrithika Santhoshini

CHAPTER TWENTY-FIVE

STRONG MAN

STRONG MEN SAY GOODBYE,
STRONGER MEN NEVER LEAVE.
M Mrithika Santhoshini

CHAPTER TWENTY-SIX

LITTLE MAN

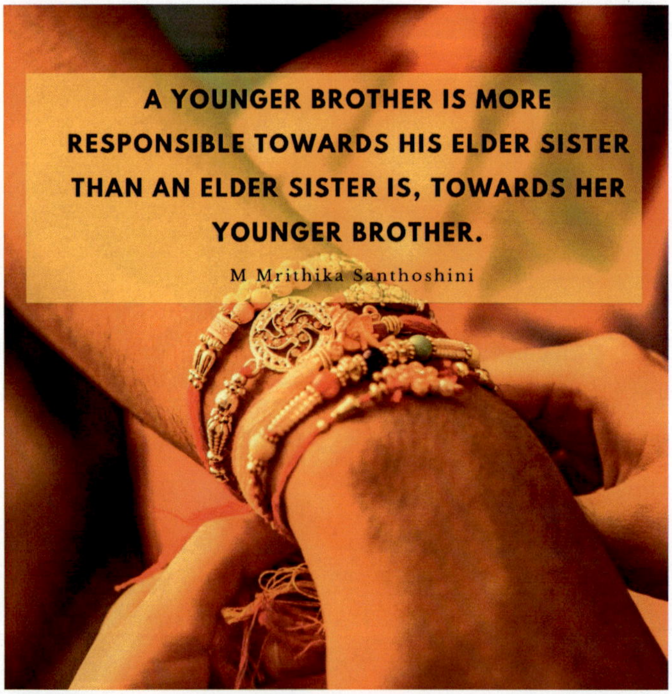
A YOUNGER BROTHER IS MORE RESPONSIBLE TOWARDS HIS ELDER SISTER THAN AN ELDER SISTER IS, TOWARDS HER YOUNGER BROTHER.
M Mrithika Santhoshini

CHAPTER TWENTY-SEVEN

DIFFERENT MAN

NO MATTER HOW OLD, A BOY IS A
MAN TO HIS MOM AND A MAN,
ALWAYS A BOY TO HIS WIFE.
M Mrithika Santhoshini

CHAPTER TWENTY-EIGHT

MIGHTY MAN

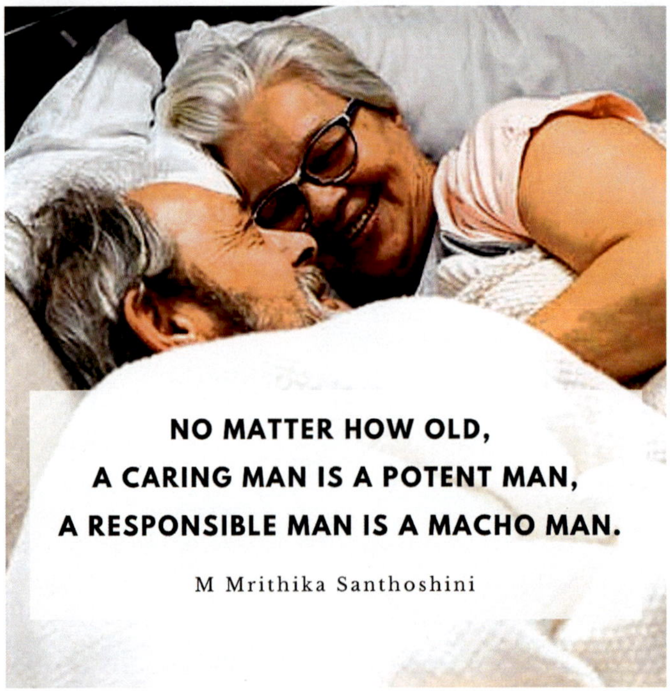
NO MATTER HOW OLD,
A CARING MAN IS A POTENT MAN,
A RESPONSIBLE MAN IS A MACHO MAN.
M Mrithika Santhoshini

CHAPTER TWENTY-NINE

MAN WITH A HEART

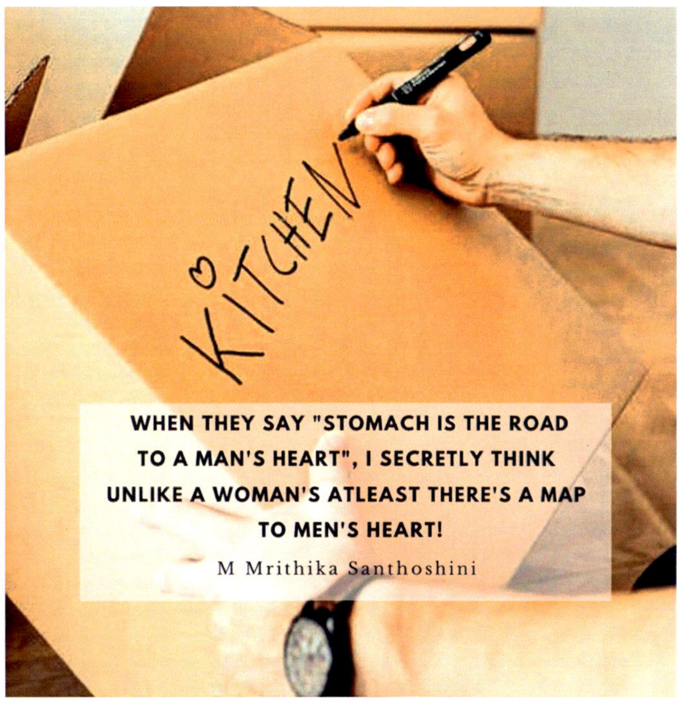
KITCHEN
WHEN THEY SAY "STOMACH IS THE ROAD TO A MAN'S HEART", I SECRETLY THINK UNLIKE A WOMAN'S ATLEAST THERE'S A MAP TO MEN'S HEART!
M Mrithika Santhoshini

CHAPTER THIRTY

OH MAN

MEN DON'T MOVE ON, THEY GROW BEARD
OR BECOME WEIRD.
M Mrithika Santhoshini

CHAPTER THIRTY-ONE

INCORRIGIBLE MAN

ROCK
WOMEN DO EVERYTHING
WHEN THE MAN LOVES HER BUT
MEN DO ANYTHING FOR THE WOMAN
WHO DOESN'T LOVE HIM BACK.
M Mrithika Santhoshini

CHAPTER THIRTY-TWO

FOODIE

MAN WHO EATS WELL
IS ALWAYS A ROMANTIC.
M Mrithika Santhoshini

CHAPTER THIRTY-THREE

MARRIED MAN

WIVES THAT SEEK COMPLETE FREEDOM FROM THEIR HUSBANDS OFTEN FORGET THAT THEY ARE CURBING HIS.
M Mrithika Santhoshini

CHAPTER THIRTY-FOUR

POOR MAN

WOMEN WHO DON'T WANT MEN TO FIND FAULT
WITH THEIR DRESSING ARE THE SAME WOMEN
WHO FINDS FAULT WITH THEIR MAN WHEN
HE DOESN'T COMPLIMENT.
M Mrithika Santhoshini

CHAPTER THIRTY-FIVE

MAN OF QUALITY

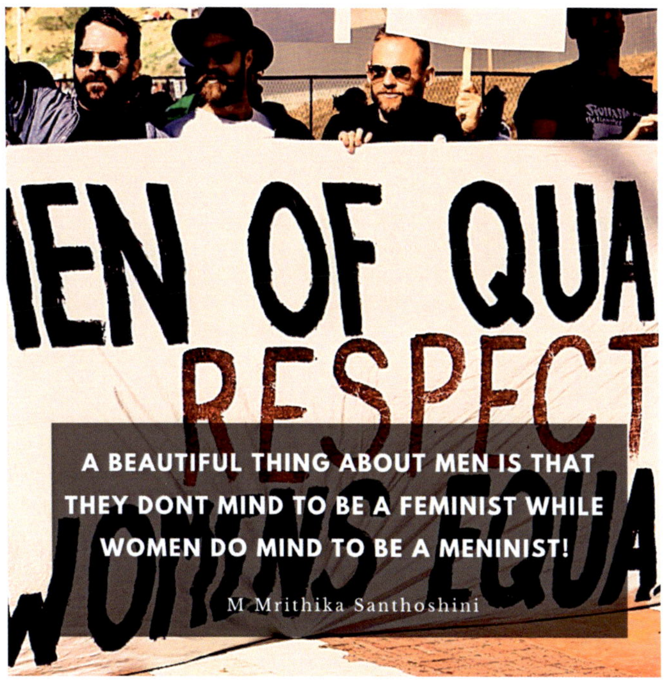

EN OF QUA
RESPECT
A BEAUTIFUL THING ABOUT MEN IS THAT THEY DONT MIND TO BE A FEMINIST WHILE WOMEN DO MIND TO BE A MENINIST!
M Mrithika Santhoshini

CHAPTER THIRTY-SIX

DANGEROUS MAN

MEN WHO COOK ARE
AS DANGEROUS AS
THE WOMEN THAT READ.
M Mrithika Santhoshini

CHAPTER THIRTY-SEVEN

TRUE MAN

M Mrithika Santhoshini
A TRUE MAN KNOWS THAT
NOT ONLY THE UNFAITHFUL WIFE,
A DISLOYAL HUSBAND IS ALSO
A BITCH.

CHAPTER THIRTY-EIGHT

GREAT MAN

GREAT MEN ARE THOSE WHO DON'T TRY TO HIDE THEIR UNGREATFUL DEEDS.
M Mrithika Santhoshini

CHAPTER THIRTY-NINE

SOME MAN

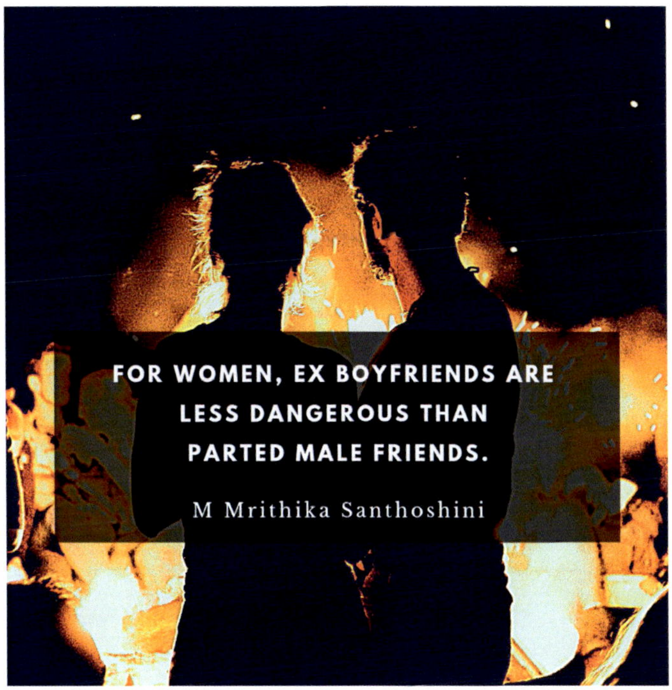
FOR WOMEN, EX BOYFRIENDS ARE
LESS DANGEROUS THAN
PARTED MALE FRIENDS.
M Mrithika Santhoshini

CHAPTER FORTY

SISSY

MAN WITHOUT CHIVALRY
IS JUST A BOY
IN HIS UNDERWEAR.
M Mrithika Santhoshini

CHAPTER FORTY-ONE

ALCOHOLIC

BEING A MAN IS A QUALIFICATION
WHICH ALCOHOLICS LOSE
IN THE PROCESS.
M Mrithika Santhoshini

CHAPTER FORTY-TWO

DISTRACTED MAN

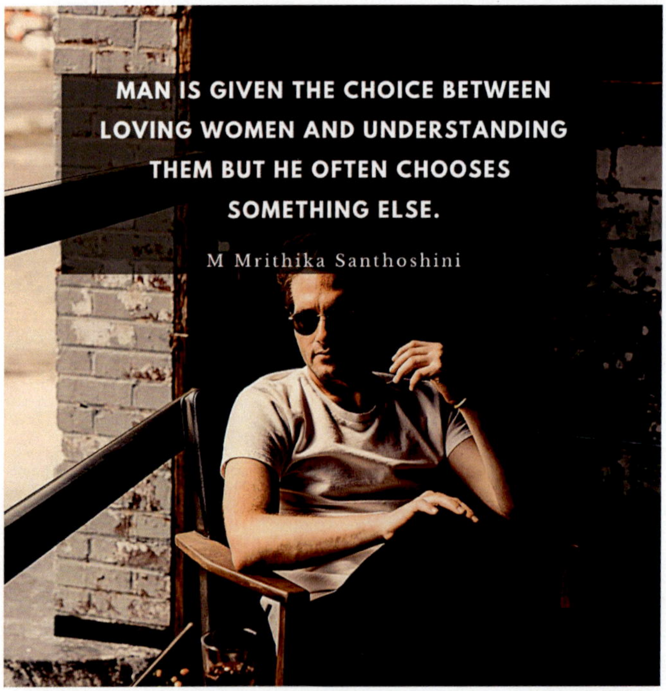
MAN IS GIVEN THE CHOICE BETWEEN
LOVING WOMEN AND UNDERSTANDING
THEM BUT HE OFTEN CHOOSES
SOMETHING ELSE.
M Mrithika Santhoshini

CHAPTER FORTY-THREE

DUMMY

MAN LOSES HIS VALUE WHEN HE TRIES TO BELITTLE THE WOMEN AROUND HIM.
M Mrithika Santhoshini

CHAPTER FORTY-FOUR

INDECENT MAN

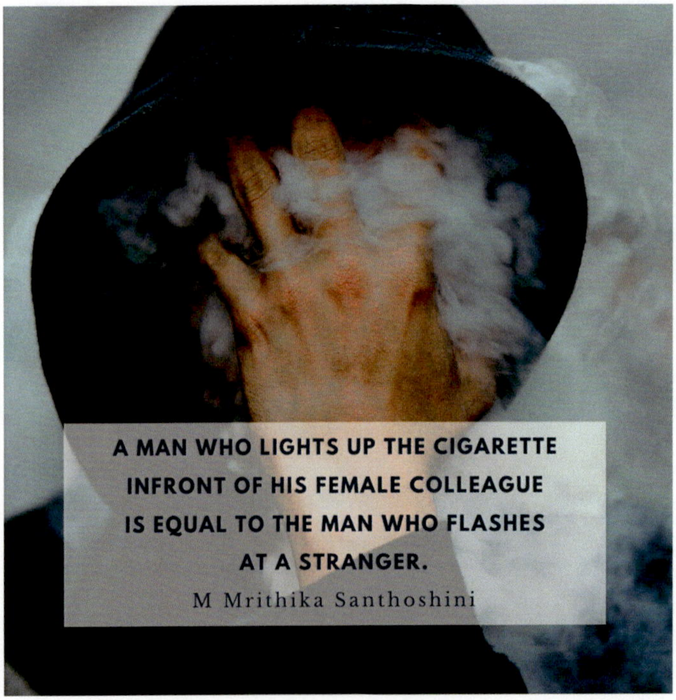
A MAN WHO LIGHTS UP THE CIGARETTE
INFRONT OF HIS FEMALE COLLEAGUE
IS EQUAL TO THE MAN WHO FLASHES
AT A STRANGER.
M Mrithika Santhoshini

CHAPTER FORTY-FIVE

NOT A MAN

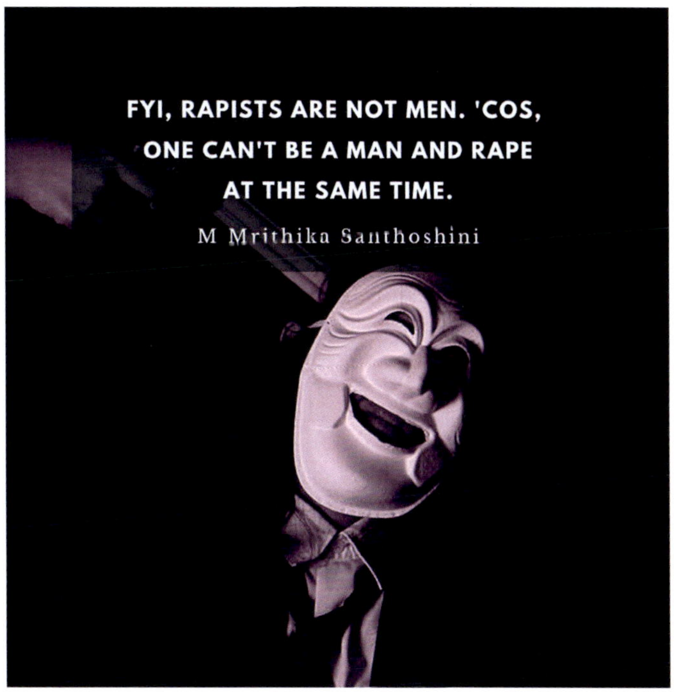
FYI, RAPISTS ARE NOT MEN. 'COS, ONE CAN'T BE A MAN AND RAPE AT THE SAME TIME.
M Mrithika Santhoshini

CHAPTER FORTY-SIX

UNMANLY MAN

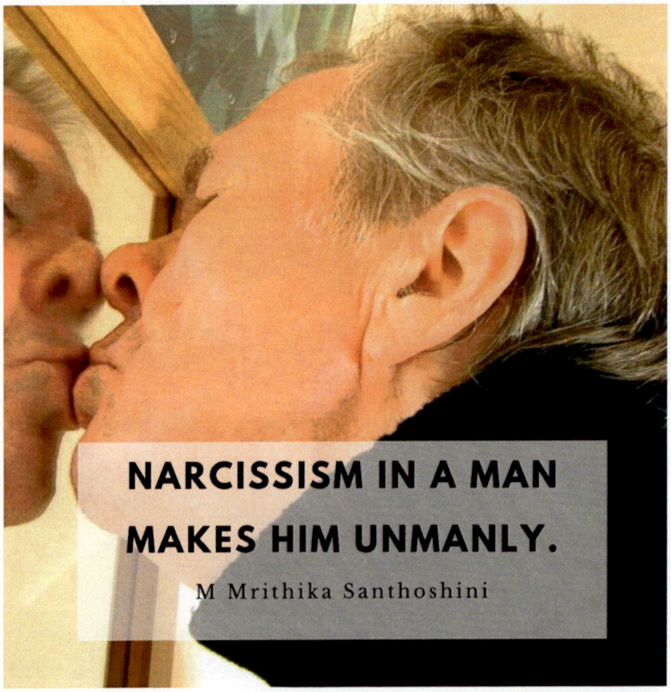
NARCISSISM IN A MAN
MAKES HIM UNMANLY.
M Mrithika Santhoshini

CHAPTER FORTY-SEVEN

COWARDLY MAN

MEN WHO DARE, PROTECT;
MEN WHO FEAR, DESTROY!
M Mrithika Santhoshini

CHAPTER FORTY-EIGHT

HOLY MAN

EVERY MAN THAT CARRIES THE SCHOOLBAG
OF HIS CHILD ON HIS BACK IS A CHRIST.
M Mrithika Santhoshini

CHAPTER FORTY-NINE

PURE MAN

THE HANDS OF A MAN WHO FEEDS
A STRAY ANIMAL IS AS DIVINE AND PURE
AS THE BREASTS OF A FEEDING MOTHER.
M Mrithika Santhoshini

CHAPTER FIFTY

HUMBLE MAN

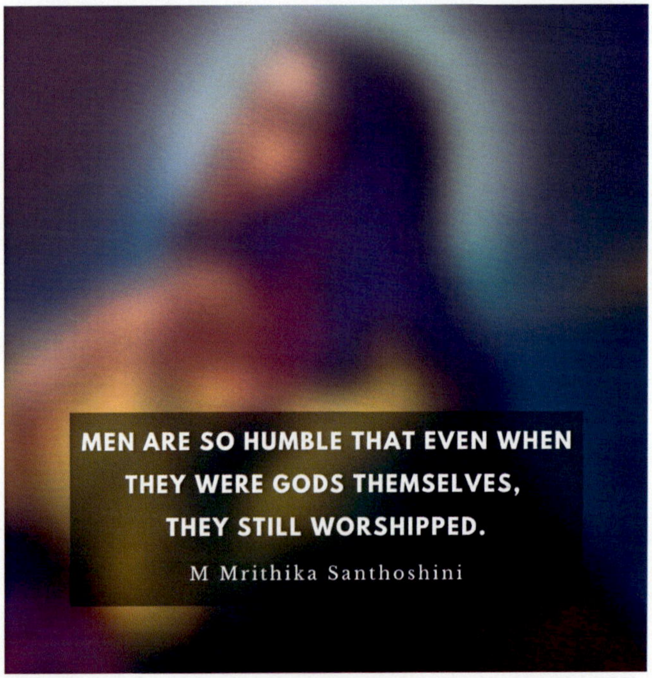
MEN ARE SO HUMBLE THAT EVEN WHEN
THEY WERE GODS THEMSELVES,
THEY STILL WORSHIPPED.
M Mrithika Santhoshini

CHAPTER FIFTY-ONE

TODAY'S MAN

MAN IS
A SOCIAL MEDIA
ANIMAL.
M Mrithika Santhoshini